WAITING
FOR THE
WRECK
TO BURN

D1416580

WAITING FOR THE WRECK TO BURN

Poems by Michele Battiste

2018 Louise Bogan Award Winner

Battiste, Michele
1ˢᵗ edition.

ISBN: 978-1-9494870-1-5
Library of Congress Control Number: 2018951420

Interior Layout & Cover Design by Lea C. Deschenes
Cover Photo: Jon Bidwell, "Birds and the Blue Sky 02"
Editing by Tayve Neese & Sara Lefsyk

Printed in Tennessee, USA
Trio House Press, Inc.
Ponte Vedra Beach, FL

To contact the author, send an email to tayveneese@gmail.com.

TABLE OF CONTENTS

1. RUINATION

2. TERROR. I MEAN RAGE.

3. *WAITING FOR THE WRECK TO BURN*

4. LINEAGE

5. TRANSITIONAL PERIOD

For Jim Kopta and Marilyn Sue Gillespie,
who are still here

1. RUINATION

RUINATION

sugar any sugar, anger every anger,
lover sermon lover, center no distractor

and the wine, and the beasts, and the butcher's raw
stock, and the bones on the floor, gnawed to artifacts.

The Y of my body, the brace of bones beneath belly, want
only want, a fractured skeleton. And your bed, and your belts,

and the view from your window, your shelf of bitters, your
shoulder a warship, two black beasts guarding the door.

One man said make yourself scarce. Hunger
feeds hunger, and the scraps aren't yours.

WEATHER REPORT FROM RUINATION

Visibility is significantly
diminished. Once there was a valley
the fog would not sink
into. Once there was a cliff
and at its edge a periscope that took
quarters. Now all the windshields steam
up as if everyone has forgotten how to work
a vent and there are no shoulders to save
us if we wander. No one is alone

in Ruination. Proximity a condition
of the weather. Always an impending
storm. Always the sudden drop
in barometric pressure that makes the beasts
restless and a body press up against another
even the inappropriate one. Much can be blamed
on weather, such as a lack of perspective.

When at the foot of a mountain it is difficult
to see anything but mountain, even
on a clear day. Ruination averages
300 days of sunshine a year. That's part
of the problem. Seeing clearly your mistake.

DESTINATION: RUINATION

Like the first unearthed bloodroot
or a black beast pacing the cattle fence—an omen.

Mama said a bird
in the hand isn't safe
from the one who holds
it. A stumble can take
anyone down, wreck
what they treasure.

One man said where some see
chance, he sees decision. Not the day
I pulled the cat off the infant
rabbit, its neck wet and red but not yet
fatal. He means the day I left. He means
the man I found.

Salvation looks like a tree flush with stone fruit, skin bursting.
Salvation looks like a man on his knees at the foot of a mountain.
Anything can look like salvation if it is not behind you.

Mama said we lose
what we leave, but no
matter. We lose
what we hide away,
lose what we save
for later.

I search the underbrush for small
wounded animals. They are not
easy to find.

The Secret of Ruination

Beneath the city lies   a labyrinth with corridors   much too
narrow for any body   bigger than a small child's.   When children disappear

      we suspect   that's where they are and worry   only slightly. We
gather near small cracks in the packed dirt to listen   for echoes, but even
      those among us   with exquisite hearing can't   be sure the sounds

      we treasure   aren't just reverberations of distant traffic.
    Those of us raised   here (we were all raised   here) remember

the labyrinth but can't picture it.   We don't know how we always
found our way   out.   How we didn't mind
the darkness.   How our lives   in the maze did not seem separate
from our lives   above ground.   We never wondered

     why our parents never mentioned it. It is an unspoken rule that we do not

     speak of it. To each other.   To outlanders.   One man outside
       our city walls went   mad from curiosity, knowing every

person could hear   sounds from cracks in the earth   that he could
   not. He set off   looking for the labyrinth.   The secret of Ruination
      is not   the labyrinth.   The secret

    is how to damn someone to Ruination without letting him in.

PREMONITION: RUINATION

Nothing happens but
dwindling. We hurt ourselves to slow
the light fading behind the pines.

The burn scabbed over, then tore, then healed. That much time
had passed.

The self speaks itself
through chosen omens: two
black beasts, bones, injury.

Maybe something sugared and silver could heal
me. Like the tongue one man said should be familiar by now.

Ruination can look like a man
on his knees at the foot of a mountain
in a certain light.

In a different light, I am simply starved and envious of the cat
with half a rabbit in her belly.

In a different light, the self-destruction did not start
when one man raised his sleepy eyes and gestured at the wine.

The light is broken – staccato flickering
at a breakneck pace.

I sip Chianti, press my thighs together beneath
the scattershot switching from darkness to illumination and back.

Two black beasts whine and grovel, pace the rooms, eye
their cages, letting me know, in their secret code, what's going on.

Denying Ruination

Two black beasts have been sent to their cages.

One has hurt her paw.

The meat is deboned and marinating.

A butcher somewhere sells soup
bones to impatient customers who swear
they will never kill.

One man once said we must make allowances
for those who find themselves
inconvenienced.

One man can't even be bothered to hold me
down.

I am no longer able to defend the warren. Today: two half
carcasses, their gray and yellow organs spill onto my step.

Helpless is something we do to ourselves when something is wrong.

I pretend nothing is wrong.

Ruination: A Case Study

I have ruined you
by leaving I have ruined you. I did not
leave and I have ruined you.

Or, the labyrinth appeared
to be something else, a trail
in the wilderness, a path
leading away. You could believe
you left Ruination, believe you could
leave this place. Or stumble upon it.

As if Ruination could be left. As if
I could ruin you by leaving

(or not). The condition of ruination is
a condition of distance. The act of ruination
is an act of separating (or its opposite).
The state of ruination is a state
of abandonment, regardless.

Perhaps you were already ruined, regardless.

To fear ruination is to believe you are
not. To believe you can be. To think
yourself worthy of ruining, different
from beasts. To not understand
the wretchedly small value
of your days.

A child. A fez. Soup bone. Belts.
A 1971 Dodge Dart. Cages
for pets who enter them eagerly.
A certain light. A different light.

To fear ruination is to suspect
it does not exist at all, that it involves
no one, that there is no reason
to worry about ~~delusions~~ omens.

It is merely the given. Like the shortest
distance between two points. You
are ruined. There is no proof.

Exhibition: Ruination

The photographer (1971 -) has pursued landscape images around the world for well over a decade. The visual drama and artistry of her photographs are born of a keen eye for the many moods of urban life.

The photographer's style is unmistakable. Her talent for rare captures of amazing and varied light imbue her opus with a sense of the epic, the majestic and the bold. Her success derives from a single-minded pursuit of the magic and energy of city streets. She often spends weeks or even months immersing herself in the setting despite the rigors of season and weather.

Awarded a grant from the Ruination City Council, the photographer returned to document the unique urban landscape of her hometown. The photos included in this exhibition were curated by the Council with an eye toward a comprehensive, integrated collection that best represents the character and shared ideals of our city.

Recognized as world-renown artist and innovator, the photographer has decided to make Ruination her permanent home after suffering a recent loss. She is a welcome addition to our community.

1. Caption: Museum of Confirmed Suspicions, note silhouette just inside gate.

2. Caption: Empty box of macarons, silver, sugar crumbs, wooden bench, City Park.

3. Caption: Municipal sculpture garden. The Y, the pit, the spinning blades, the diorama of man, his knees, North Mountain.

4. Caption: West border wall.

5. Caption: Mauled rabbit, digestive organs. A common sight.

6. Caption: Unlicensed noodle house run by a matriarchal line traced to the city's founders. The women listen to cracks between cobblestones, refuse to speak.

7. Caption: Black beasts guarding City Hall. Appear ferocious but have taken to licking ankles as children pass.

8. Caption: Fencing along southern border. Notice how the photographer captures slight glitches in camouflage, the liminal space between barrier and background.

9. Caption: Shadow birds escape the plaza wall, haul away creator's hands. Not captured: vicious caws.

10. Caption: Public school yard and adjacent woodlands. Missing children often appear emerging from the trees quite dirty but unharmed and in good spirits.

11. Caption: Union Street between 7th and 8th Boulevards—Clinic, Oscar's Meats, Chamber of Commerce, Office of Tourism, Department of Immigration, the Stumble Inn, Sticky Sweet Shop, Green Star Dry Cleaning, Green Star Grocery, Eloise's Extermination Service.

12. Caption: East River and skyline of bordering town. Good rivers make good neighbors.

Ruination: Variation

The self demands a new creation
myth, a mass of particles
that haven't yet

        lined up,
making all things possible
again. The man at the foot of the mountain, not

fallen, not supplicating, just there
for a moment before he rises, moves
away.

    It was me who wanted
to reconstruct the ruins I
abandoned, no maze that led me

here, though I told myself
I was lost, though I pretended
to be careful

      with the bird
I carried. One man said I was pointlessly,
effortlessly cruel. Which is another

                possibility.
Yesterday I ran the fields
with two black beasts, mindless

of what we trampled.
We have always loved
each

    other as siblings, envious
of the others' access to scraps,
bones, keeping

       the gate. We know
this place by smell, by what
we have broken, detritus still

lying about. It is how we stake
our claim of worthless territory.
It is how we claim

                it is not
ruined. Today I saved another
rabbit from the cat. We were both

terrified. I wondered what would happen
next.

RUINATION CITY COUNCIL

The standards have been approved.
The clever ones can find their way
around them. Already lawsuits
are clogging the courts but no
one expects resolution, just
drama. Just posturing. Just making
sure personal opinion is considered
when legislating. There are

formulas. Algorithms. Who has
curfews who is allowed to leave who
is forced out how high the walls.
Ordinances regulating the keeping
of wild animals and the proper storage
of bones. The accuracy of maps.
The definition of melodrama. The definition
of threats to local security. Court orders:

*Get off the floor. Go home and bake
brownies for Christ's sake. Eat some
soup. Pet your dogs. Get a manicure.
You aren't ruined. Your feelings
are hurt. Stop your keening before we show
you what ruined really looks like.*

Ruination

As a matter of course, ruined most often follows
abandoned, but ask the mangled family
of rabbits and they'll tell you
there is a distinct collapse beneath a specific
kind of attention. Their blood trails
like hieroglyphics on my steps. I'm not mourning
your leaving. I'm mourning the mess
I make flailing about, small pieces
missing, holes leaking a telltale fluid. And you
standing up from your knees, walking
to the river. It may be enough. To be indelible.

Where the Darkness is Never Filtered

Who could have known
after you cleaned
up, started wearing
that fez around
Lark Street and upped
the Thorazine
that you would look
so *good*. I would

have wrestled you,
drove around all
night with your
cigarettes scumming
the windshield of my
grandmother's '71 Dodge Dart
if it could change
the future had
I known the future
was a river
you would stumble
into.

Your voice laid
down rails I would have
followed anywhere.
Mostly night. Mostly
tunnel burrowing
underground, always
a howl echoing
faintly and I
imagined beast
answering unseen
beast. You brought me
to the border
of Ruination
every night and
pretended you could
not see beyond
the tree line. Or maybe

you could not see
beyond the tree line.

Which is how I learned
that the future was to few
people's taste, that they
had to fish out
your body, that
the darkness is nothing
to be afraid of,
only the morning.
Its certain light.

A Mechanistic Understanding
of the Systems in which it Works

Think about
of those who reach
denial. (Where) you
Even if you cross. Choose
or the other. Mourn this side
Suddenly. But a river is
you can be inside
the river is to be in
Maybe this
and maybe you weren't
But even a child knows
to cross

the border. What it asks
it. Its immediate
cannot be.
one loss
or that.
a border
of. To never leave
between always.
is what you thought
wrong.
what it means
over. You crossed

over in the river. The night air
a light jacket the waterlogged weight of it
holding you. The river was nowhere

near Ruination. It was just
brown and misused river
the town. It was years
I could be on one
of a border and the border
destroy me, only take
side. I can build
the beasts, worry
me as I leave,
is that I do not think
you, only how you
Saved

a simple
that cut
ago and I knew
or the other side
would not
away the other
a fire, smack
the town will curse
but the way this works
of saving
could have waited.
me.

Ruination || Ruination

Why, when you brought me to the edge
of Ruination, could you not

cross? You knew the way, the secret
tunnels that bypassed

border guards. But you always surfaced
early, surprised to find yourself still
here. Because you were already

ending. To be ruined means you must go

on. Which in a certain light could be seen
as salvation. In a different light you were a risk

I should have taken.

The riverbank where they laid your body was nothing
special. The edge of a border that had nothing
to divide for no reason. Your story is less

about Ruination and more about this town
where you stopped and I continued.

The ghosts that ride slow freight cars across the rail bridge
high above the river, getting to nowhere but pick

and spade, large machines. The boathouse keeper only half
damaged by stroke rolling across the grass to reach the pier.

Each new decorative fountain.

No one in this town knows we border Ruination
but they fear it's true and make decisions

accordingly. When you died I thought
I narrowly missed the worst of it. That the worst

of it was over. You know what they call this town from the other side of the wall?

They call this town Ruination.

Spite House

It's not what you would
remember if you weren't
dead. Bits of sky missing, peripheries
eroded. White, unnecessary pillars. Gazebos
sporadic throughout municipal grounds.
They dredged the river. They dammed
the river. A decorative fountain
where the house everyone hated
stood. Everyone looked away.

Everyone thought best to change.
Detective Moskowitz stopped
trading favors with Italians and the town
paved over the path through
the woods. It is smooth and wide
and the townsfolk are jolly. No
one boils escarole. No one notices
the shifting. The lack of local
celebrities. The secret conduits.

When I say everyone hated the house
I mean it was condemned. It was
demolished tastefully. Taking
into account its proximity to a well-lit
intersection. The family received
a check. You would remember
the son. In school he was quiet but not
ashamed. After school we snuck
to his house and leaned heavily
against the siding, stared at the others
who came, chose who we wanted.

The town council thought a fountain
had more teeth than a bench. Sent a message
of what will and will not be tolerated.
The family was not indifferent. The river had
many locks then. It still cannot be disciplined.

Some say they left their house standing
out of spite. I say we are lucky to be
left standing and everyone knows
where they went.

Nowhere Near (Ruination)

You can't come here. Where rivers are choked
with stormwater. Where stormwater escapes
the sewers. Where sewers define a border we prefer

not to think about. So everywhere
else. Where roads. Where gardens. Where circulars
bring added value to less engaged members of the community.

Where birdsong fails to rouse the sleepers. Where rain turns
to stormwater and weeps its degradation in foamy runoff. It weeps
as it poisons the trout. It weeps as it poisons insensible toads. You see

what can happen. How berries mold. How bees turn
placid, lose their way home. But the streets
are rinsed clean. The unfortunate

and the fortunate together clutch their circulars
on their way to the store. You can't come here. You
have your own river in the shadow of Ruination.

Which may be preferable. If you had a choice.

GETINTHERIVERGETINTHE
RIVERGETINTHERIVERGET

When they pulled you from the water
filled with stones. When they
the water,
turned blue. Bathtub drains
above them. The wind blew
the east from the north from
down at the river.
the water
dreamed a fountain
A child said in death
All things are home.
in the river.
in the river.
in the river.

their pockets
pulled you from
mothers' lips
tugged menacingly at the bodies
from the south from
the west dying
When they pulled you from
a child
in the center of town.
all things are equal.
A child said get back
I told the child I was never
A child said get back
Quick.

2. TERROR.
I MEAN RAGE.

ONCE MORE, WITH FEELING

Of course   I am to die
    on a Thursday.   The sky −
wide   through the windows   −   mocks
             the locked door.   Our eyes   wild
track clouds   bloated   from a
         binge   of afternoon.   They
amble   past the frame.   We
crouch beneath   desks.   I
     mean,   students crouch beneath
      desks. Smart   these students.   Quick
and young.   When gunshots cracked
     the air I rose   wandered
      the room   to vanish   faced
   an impartial   corner,
            the inevitable
       fate.   Marilyn Sue, I'm
    talking   to you   nine days
        after they found you   three
  days   dead.   Of course I will
be slaughtered   counting sins
     in the corner of a
     classroom   the door shut and
     locked by the handsome one
         before he slipped beneath
his desk.   I have lusted
hated   stolen   cheated
     and the gunman   knows.   Did
   you know   Sue?   The knife? Your
    neck?   Was there time to count
     your children   speak names
        regret?   Or were you just
confused?   I move behind
       a cabinet of books.
     Erin creeps.   Whispers her
    escape route. The windows
     where sky beckons   mocks
our little   fear.   Anyone but
    me   I breathe   pressing her

hand   knowing my luck is

                            bad.   *The window*, Erin

says   and I   blank.   The gun

              barrel will follow   my

     back like a husband's   gaze.

                I rummage for my son's

face   lock it down   and back

             inside   my uterus

     to die with him   intact.

            The sky   remains   outside

   the glass.   The gunman can

            turn   right

                       or left.

AFTERSHOCK

The building hushed
its bricks. We heard no cries
or shrieks. Construction
in the room above.
Roofing gun on tin,

the echo, stilled. That
was it. The cops took
statements. The students
left to drink and text.
Of course, tragedy

does not end with Sue.
The sky remains
outside the glass. I
would have sacrificed
them all.

Locus Amoenus

Marilyn Sue sinks to her kitchen floor like a goose in tall grass before it
knows it has been stoned to death by children, and the garden disappears.
Gone like the 8x10 print of the photo I told her I'd make and never did.
Not that I never did, I just haven't yet. There is always time, there just
stops being reason to fill it. Let me explain. My son says, *I want too much.*
More than he's been allotted or promised. Bedtime milk or pudding. I
don't want more time. I want a garden. Sue fattened the hydrangea like a
Christmas duck grown beloved and named. Her bamboo scratched at the
sky in a blind search for the gate. What I'd be taking on. Opportunities
for ruin and neglect. I am good at cursing frost. Feeling conflicted about
beetles. Pruning away the worm-eaten and the dead. I have no skill
with the root or tendrils. Prefer to ignore their creeping implications. A
fruitless accounting, my proficiencies and defects. When the lottery came
up for a community plot, I refused to enter. When my son asks for too
much he already knows the answer. Why he craves what sickens him, what
gives him pain in the night.

In the House

I won't quote statistics.
He knows and counters with
inverted numbers, spin,
the same skillfully wrought
manipulations of
fact my sources offer,
but other sources, the
other side: *More children*
die in family pools
than by gunshot wounds. Should
I forbid our son to
visit your mother's house
because your parents had
to have that damn pool? He

is smart and terrified.
An unlocked door. The dark.

The empty house begging
every lunatic and
David Golden to come,
enter, crouch in the blind
corner, gouge ragged holes
in linoleum with
a stiff boning knife while
waiting, and wait for
what's
left of my husband's (wife
sister daughter son that's
it) kindred to trust
their
day to continue the days
before. So a glock. A
.38. Bullets in
the dresser. A safe on
the closet floor. Beneath
the bed, targets riddled
by a shaking, inept
hand.

33

                                        I've moved away
from reason   as you would
            expect.   I yell and weep
            and threaten   nothing worth
      losing and   he know my
arsenal   is empty.

                              Talk to me when your own
                              fucking mother is stabbed
                              to death.   And later, when
            he's calm,   *What if David*
                            Golden broke into our
                            home?   You already know
my answer,   the one my
                  brilliant but terrified
                              husband should have
                              reasoned
            out himself.   I tell him,
                  He already did.

ONE METHOD OF AVOIDANCE

Let's have a baby. Let's
have a baby. Let's have
another baby. Come on,
let's have another. Come
on, people, let's have a baby
now. Come on, people now,
let's. Smile. A baby. Smile
on each baby. Let's have
another baby now. Now smile
on your. Brother, a baby. Everybody,
let's have another. Everybody,
get together, let's have a baby.
Get together, try and love.
Another baby. Let's have
another baby. Let's have one
another now. Come on, people
now, smile on your brother,
everybody get together, try and
love one another. Right now.
Let's have a baby. Right now.
Let's have a girl baby. Let's
name her. Right now. Marilyn Sue.

THE COOK'S TEMPTATION

Cast iron: iconic. Romantic
even. Well-oiled. Seasoned. But far
too heavy. Fatal surely. If wielded
with. Determination or luck.

Stainless steel. Core: aluminum.
Progressive: even heat distribution.
And yet. Too much heft despite mass
production. Deceptive, a brushed metal

sheen. Dollar store purchase. Metal:
aluminum. Condemned: dementia.
Shoved to the back of the shelf. Burns
easy. A dent from each hardy scrub. It will

do. For striking. My husband's
head. Emphasis or attention. Or
defense. A wallop but. No lasting
damage. This his how I choose

a pan for the stir fry. Some minds.
The proximity (necessity, option)
of weapons. This is why. I plead
(threaten). No guns in the house.

Remains

Five acres
by land no
your father's.
schoolhouse
married, my
already
his fists
womb. The gate
up with
broom grass,
a path to
The neighbor's
escaped
the dirt
giving up
their run
This is the
saved, the
of your planned
when the world
nuts. Sue,
license plates,
toothbrush
son. My
to put aside
butcher's block
You know what
avoiding:
in the box
the bureau.
not home.
safe. Nothing
like you
remains:
I mean
Terror. I

bordered
longer
The stone
that saw you
husband
waving
inside your
knotted
overgrown
guarding
the creek.
goats have
their pen, crossed
road always
dust, have
of the place.
land you
asylum
escape
goes
we have your
the red
you bought my
husband thought
the
I loved.
I am
ashes
on top
You are
We are not
ended
wanted. What
the trial.
pilgrimage.
mean rage.

FRENCH TOAST AFTER NOON

The best luck of all is not
to survive. The best luck is not
to be left behind. In other words,
to be haunted. I don't know what
I'm talking about—assuming
what the dead want when the dead
don't matter. I should stop. Leave
this argument alone or to
theologians. The theologians
want solitude and there I go
again. Assuming. To be left
behind is a death of sorts. But
to be haunted is to be dreamt
of in reverse. A reclamation.
Of sorts. What I'm talking about
is mourning damnable luck.
The need to be claimed. A nod
in this direction. The dead,
they let that go. The dead, they
are too disillusioned to
bother. They climb mountains
to get to the other side. *This is
how we descend,* they say, not
caring if anyone watches. I'll
tell you a story. Louis',
a diner wedged cliffside above
the Sutro Baths, the ocean
frolicking below, hoarse from
shouting *Look at me! Look at
me!* Iris, near eighty, plastic
violets in her hair held by
plastic barrettes. There's a game
we played hung over: attempt to
order French toast as the sun sets.
The gamble – Iris takes
the order, her gaze indulgent
and impatient, or she huffs,
points to the sign above
the counter: "NO French Toast

After Noon." That Iris, we
laugh and poke each other
whether our luck is good or
bad. The best, when she points
and brings it anyway. It
mattered. Fifteen years ago. Iris
died. Does she care I'm writing
this? She doesn't care.

3. WAITING FOR THE WRECK TO BURN

AMERICAN PROVERB: KISSING A GIRL BECAUSE SHE IS WILLING IS LIKE SCRATCHING A PLACE THAT DOESN'T ITCH.

The rain hovers but refuses.

Children drag toes in the dust, raising pitiable
ghosts, ignoring torn skin when a spiked
vine finds them.

It lets the blood come out the smallest one
tells the others.

A backhoe gores the pocked macadam of the lot.
The earth beneath leaks its scent of anther and crypt.

The smallest eyes the clouds she thinks she is
breathing.

Please, she begins to pray, then begins again. *I will wait.*

PREPARING THE CHILD

Copperheads, fanatics, power tools
in disrepair, the one who tortures
bugs (and you might try it
once, a small stab at easy cruelty,
and for that I'll wish on you

a minor emotional trauma) all easy
to avoid. Check for patterns, twitches,
rust, glints. Worth your dread
are the tricky evils, the devil's small
scratches along a spine, provoking

an itch impossible to pinpoint,
more difficult to name. Even symptoms
are misleading, often mistaken
for vision or defense. I can only warn
you that faith won't save you,

nor a finely-wired intellect, nor
the broad, enlightened upbringing
we had planned. This family has a mediocre
relationship with chance, but good
enough. You'll be that blessed.

An Accounting of an Entomological (and, at times, a Malacological) Persuasion

Once, I harbored a spider.   I felt
                    big-hearted.
                                        I came home and found
dozens of her babies   on my kitchen ceiling.   I stood
                    on a chair   and with the pad of my thumb
                    I crushed them all.

      *   *   *

It's never too late to realize
insects are happier
outdoors.   So after I shook
                    the millipede
                    from the drapes
                    my mother gave me

          I chased it
          across the floor
          and trapped it
          beneath a cup.   My aim was bad.
                              I severed several legs
                              from its body.

They spasmed like ghost limbs
that were not ghosts.

      *   *   *

One night I pointed out a slug on the sidewalk, alerting my friend to its size.
It was a small animal. My friend squashed it with his shoe. Said it was bad
for gardens. We were nowhere near a garden.

      *   *   *

I let my son   sit on the ground   to trace crooked
    paths in the dirt   with his finger   for the ants. They
climbed his body   and stung   his tiny neck.

                    *   *   *

            Sometimes,   in the old apartment
      on 29ᵗʰ Street,   confused
                flour beetles would find their way
            into   the hot pepper flakes.   When I
      sprinkled hot pepper
                      into the soup
confused flour beetles   fell from the jar.
                    They died.   I fished
            them out and   did not tell
      my husband.   For Christ's   sake.
        I had spent   an hour   on that soup.

                    *   *   *

            I suspect
            wasps have built a nest
            in the eave above our balcony.
            I will not bother them. I will seek
            professional help.

                    *   *   *

When we were dating, my husband
built a fire on the bank of Fall
River. A swarm of mayflies threw
themselves into the flames. The thin
cylinders of their abdomens

snapped like wet kindling. We thought
it was an omen, these small
beings that flung themselves into
the fire and made a pleasant
dying sound. The marriage has been,

at times, very rough.

When the Light Falters

The moon is out
of practice. A

small broken stone.
The closed window.

The serrated edge of the neighboring
roof confuses me. Blocking sky as if we are sewn

inside a seam.

The closed window creaks there
is no wind the serrated
edge of the roof. I am not

young enough
to pretend

the circumstances are better. The night

is clammy. We breathe
the same air and suffer

from it. I crave
saltwater as if

that is all that is denied to me.

Nothing swells or pulls
toward the moon. A

small broken stone. What moon
cannot illuminate

a perilous edge either
at my feet or looming? Your

moon. Your blind-spotted, petulant,
hand-wringing moon.

CONFESSIONAL

Forgive me for being forty-one, married, a good
mother, a bad wife. I've fallen for a twenty-two year

old Moroccan cashier who quotes Moliere,
wasting precious family time to invent scenarios

that lead to an unintended kiss. With tongue.
Tiny nips. A finger grazing clavicle, a hand hooked

inside belt. I'll get over it and dream it all over
again: a shy Scottish banker, a lazy cowboy

with the shakes. At twenty, I was disarmed
by a boy of fifteen at a rented beach house

in Lavallette. My brother shamed me
into avoiding every scenario I could invent.

That boy is now thirty-six with a hole in his
memory the shape of my mouth. My husband is a good

man I sometimes hate. I don't take calls
from the high school beau who traced

circles on my spine the last time we met.
But once I did. Found a bench in the sun

and let his suggestions break my oaths again
and again. I lie. I'm a good wife who can't help

inviting tragedy to lurk in every corner.
This is not a story. As if all of my stories are true.

Almost Adulterer's Guide to Menu Planning

When I cook with wine, I am thinking of another man.
When I cook with the good wine, I think, *any other man but you.*
When I drink the wine I'm cooking with, I'm putting forth
    the effort to be present.
When I melt butter and lick it off a plate, I've been neglected.
When I omit anchovies from the *puttanesca,* I resent
    your particular tastes.
Any time I put salsa on everything, I should have just licked melted butter
    off a plate.
When I toast the meatball subs until the cheese is bubbling, I am appealing
    to the part of you that prefers to live alone.
When I make a chili, don't call it a stew.
When I make gazpacho, don't call it a stew.
When I make a stir-fry, don't call it a stew.
When I spoon cottage cheese into the baby's mouth, I remember
    the night you made Hungarian pasta three years ago.
When I make kaposztas teszta, my mother makes it better.
When I make umborkasalata, my mother makes it better.
When I make macaroni salad, I remember when you told my mother
    that my macaroni salad was better than hers.
When dried salami and head cheese are hidden in the crisper, my mother
    is coming for a visit. She knows about our menu, I have sunk that low.
When I put blackberries in the pancakes, I am pleasing you.
When I put blueberries in the pancakes, I am pleasing me.
I don't make stew.
When I read the cookbook, I am trying to remember.
I microwave frozen burritos when the marriage is doomed.
I heat canned tomato soup when the marriage is doomed.
When I refuse to acknowledge a doomed marriage, I add carrots, celery,
    tortellini and hope it is enough.
When I use the measuring spoons, I don't trust myself.
When I bake cookies from cake mix, they are often for someone else.

When I roast the root vegetables I wish someone else would roast
   the root vegetables.
When I wash the dishes, I wish you would get off your ass and wash the dishes.
When I make strawberry rhubarb crumble, it is summer and I almost
   believe you find me lovely.
When I pan-fried peaches in butter and brown sugar, it was summer and I
   was in love.
When I cooked who knows what in lingerie and heels, it was summer and
   you asked.
When I make stuffed peppers, I am staring at the last ditch.
When I read the cookbook, I am trying to remember.
When I price the snow peas, I am thinking of another man, the one who
   tends a garden, the one who mixes dressing, the one who cooks with
   ginger for the heat.

DOMESTICITY

The labor of staying
is similar to the labor
of not screaming outside
your mouth. In other words,

it's work to keep
the swallowed keens
and screeches swallowed.
Fuck you, you'd like

to gently and civilly
reply, your clenched fist
so effervescent with middle
finger it floats to the end

of your reach, hovers
and shakes when no one
is looking and rarely
does anyone look. Think

of a child's fist, filled
with treasure and dexterous
enough to grab more.
You have forgotten

to grab what you
value and find yourself
stroking a ladle,
wondering at its ability

to sink then surface
so heavy with muchness,
more than you ever
thought it could hold.

18 Days Before Solstice

sounds like I'm about to wax ecological, perhaps begin
with pellucid ice melting off a stone bench in the garden,
but the truth is these days I chase down the sun and stand
before it like an only child anxiously gauging
its unreliable and mostly inadequate parent.

Today it sets at 4:36 but will disappear
behind the mountain at 3:31 as if it can't stand
me, and already I'm thinking how the darkness wears
me down and has me eating frosting out of a can.
From a stone bench in the garden I watch crows skim

the partly frozen pond as if the water beneath wouldn't kill them,
which may suggest that I'm depressed but the truth is
I'm angry. It's not fair to imply a daring and enviable
life when you are simply hungry or bored or cold.
And I don't understand how I got here: standing before

a celestial body begging for more and counting days
until we can move past this relentless accounting,
this determination of what is due and what is wasted
and what is coming, all of us skimming the edge
of calamity pretending it can never happen, not to us.

Scorpedo to the Rescue

We will say we love
each other. We will
show him the moon
from different places
and tell him that it is
the same moon. We
will divide his books,
forget the stories
we have given up.
We will say absence
is not different than
distance. We pretend
there is no absence.
We will pretend that
nothing broke, there are
no chasms, we are not
scared, that nothing will
again be lost
as easily as the
bottle cap he tossed away
then bitterly mourned.
We will buy new toys
again and again.
We believe his joy
cannot be lost no
matter how hard we
throw it. I searched
everywhere for what
I knew was worthless.
Then I stood before
the display of Hot
Wheels and picked the one
with a scorpion's
tail. *This one,* I'll say, *goes
faster than all the others.
Nothing* I will say
is better.

MACHINES ARE FOR LEAVING

Your brother used up all the drama. Your father
swallowed all the crumbs. My sister used up all
the pity. The bicycle is broken. The turbine

is down. Your mother used up all the reason.
My mother reinvented scorn. The others
failed to thrive waiting for the wreck

to burn. Let's sleep you say through each
collision, nothing toxic nothing that would
risk escape. We could live justly in the ruins.

We could ossify beneath the ash. No one
will relinquish currency. No one cuts
us any slack. We could trace each other's

torsos, redundant vessels too heavy
to shift. We could leave with nothing just
start walking but I have used up all the grace.

4. LINEAGE

O. Uva

Turquoise should not be worn
by the faint-hearted, those who shy away
from a resemblance between the grape and the egg.
To be redolent is asking for it. Better
to run off with the unborn than to hide
in the nest.

Cojones, sister?
Admit it. When you were twelve you slipped
two boiled eggs into a sandwich bag to know
what balls feel like. Put on the damn
stones and wolf down your breakfast: pulp, skin
and seed. You'll need your strength.

O. Turquoise

You have been
warned. The lonely male.
Grape-shaped stones on a
string. The polish is too bright.
Lines of sard recollecting
ground. A whine like something
icy spills, then breaks. The string
was just a thread. The man is
just. To treasure the sard is to be
redolent. Don't misunderstand
me. We ovulate and crave *la
tierra*, and sister, we are thirsty.
The *vino* tastes of the loam
that birthed it, the region
that sent it away.

O. You Have Been Warned

On his knees, my son. Says "look mama, *uva*." His face
gleams, holds up a bead as big as my thumb. The sun had not
shone for hours. No one warned me. The string was just

a thread. To persist is to treasure the sard. Sister,
we miss your silver hair. The light is enough. My son lies
on the ground, sucks the dirt off his *uva*. Remember

the uncle who tapped a hole in the shell, sucked out
the yolk? *Él fue un mutante.* My son drifts, the stone
hidden in his fist, slick as the kept firstborn.

O. On His Knees

Whether or not he had broken

he suckled. Whether the wine

the stones were found. To let go

El *óvulo* is fertile, whether

Mi hermana, whether or not,

the string. Whether or not

was spilled or not. Whether

the drops of blood is to persist.

or not. Skin, seed and pulp.

we are just.

O. WEATHER

Wool and   briar patch.   Bees.   An overgrowth of
sage.   Sister,   we missed the path, the land
that sent us   away.   The goats are tied up,
far from the grape vine.   They strain.   Little
steps,   little steps   you tell   me, hunting
through nests. One twig   is sharp.
Tener hambre   is   to let go the drops
of *sangre.*   We find one,   small as a stone,
the color of   creek.   The color of
                 sky.

O. Wool

La uva está adentro de la boca de mi hijo.
La uva es una piedra. The string,
no wonder it broke. No wonder the man
is just waiting. Sister, let's drink. Let's
hoard. We *miss la tierra de nuestras ancianas.*
To be asking is to be hungry. Our son
was born in a nest of wool. We bled. We
were greedy. We pine for other eggs.
We mend the string. We string the stones.

5. TRANSITIONAL PERIOD

Life on Pluto

There are those among us who refuse
to memorize the planets in their proper
order. Once a man attended the council
meeting and spoke of monetizing

our collateral. We knew him
for a stranger but coveted the fine
stitching on his boots. As if his roads
were all and always freshly paved but smelled

nothing of cooling asphalt. Some say
this town is awfully cold but none
of us know what weather is.
Though we think we do, like a born-blind

child knows the color silver is a sudden
squall across a tarn and shuddering
nearby aspens. The bread at the bakery
tastes like moss and the baker says, *nom*

nom nom as she hands out samples. We feel
only pity for her and for each other.
We know what pitiful is. A shadow
growing longer despite the orbit

of five moons. We know night.
A shadow raging to be released
from its shell. The watchman knows
our names and keeps us in check. Dissuades

us from thinking of others. When we cross
each other's path we hiss because
we know love. Someone once came to us
and spoke gently of the Pleiades.

That is it, we whispered. A constellation
we can refer to. Like silver. Like the sun
that, when it finally comes, makes
the shadows small.

AMERICAN PROVERB: WHAT A WOMAN DOESN'T KNOW, SHE IMAGINES.

The fall from the balcony, not so
bad. What survives on a regular
basis: sticks, shoes, plastic cups,
anything metal. Anything sharp

stays sharp, though it may bend.
Most objects are worth retrieving.
Some appear valuable from great
or even mediocre heights. One

night she stands on a chair. One
night she leans over the railing.
One thing she knows though no
one told her. What we've lost is also

what we desire.

Impending

When the storm moves away, as I do.
When the storm   touching.
When the hand is leading.
When the hand   the light.
When the eye takes what it wants.
When the eye   and not touching.
The hand between slats of a chair back.
The eye releases   the light.
When the storm shakes the portico
this thigh that thigh   are the same.
(The storm
  is a bloodthirsty   thing.)
When the mouth, without effort, claims.
When the storm approaches
touching the light and not touching
the light are the same thing.

Conditional Guidelines
for the Transitional Period

Stop having the conversation.

Once I saw a woman dive through the hole a man made
with his arms. Take note of the consequences. They are particular
to the transitional period.

The part about the celebrity lover. Leave that part out.

Pretend this is not a transitional period, but do not pretend
this is after the transitional period. The only acceptable
period to acknowledge is the time before the transitional period.

When you lose the ring don't ask, *Want to hear something
ironic?*

Make note of durable vertical surfaces—a building's rough
brick, car doors, the smooth bark of old birch trees—in case
you have no place to go when in the transitional period.

You have no place to go in the transitional period.
Every shelter is inadequate.

In that case, everything depends on the elements. Spring
is best for the transitional period, seeing as how it mimics
disappointment.

Make no demands. That sort of certainty during
the transitional period is inappropriate.

Wear sensible foundation garments. No one needs
to be getting any ideas.

Scratch that. The transitional period is the best time
to purchase something sheer or vinyl for when
the transitional period ends.

You will become unexpectedly drowsy in the middle
of the transitional period.

Sometimes you will attempt to escape desire.

Desire is inescapable throughout the transitional period.
Desire is inextricably tied to the effort of escaping.

Desire is inextricably tied to mourning.

Desire is tied to lack. You cannot escape this whether or not
you are in or out of the transitional period.

Backwater Rising

Backwater rising, baby, come on.
There's panic in the landscape.
What one glitch in hindsight reveals,
what one broadcast made us
believe, come on. Gather
the fractures of your self can't be
recovered though you
stutter, frozen there. The aperture
like a wound, your split
lip messy with fluid
and nothing will be perceived
undamaged again.
Each movement threatens
a gap to let the water
in. How stupid we were
to feel safe. We blink
the incremental
rising, risks dismissed
as minute, pieced together
like this. What mistaken faith holds
the landscape—I see now—lashed
together, the water
rising, your lashes the first
chaos. Leave it, baby, we cannot
be again the whole of it going
under, *come on*.

A Few Words of Appreciation

Thank you for choosing me. Thank
you for choosing to study anatomy, for
differentiating between a fever and a minor
disturbance, a small misunderstanding, a passing
whim. You have a dog and so you can tell
intuitively as well as scientifically. When attention
wanes. When anyone else will do. When a breastbone
is no different from any other breastbone and when
a breastbone will never release you, not until
you've gnawed it to shards that scratch your throat
going down.

Thank you for your discretion. Thank
you for the porkpie hat pulled low so no one
can guess which gaze is avoidable. I appreciate
your lack of actualization, your double whiskey
restraint, which is surprising. You've not sent
signal, which others may read as disinterest,
but once I had a cat.

Thank you for occasionally sitting
next to me, for the brush of thigh when you shift
away. I snuck my hairclip into your pocket.
It's cruel to deny the tension, to breathe
casually, to refuse you the rare scent
of encouragement.

Thank you for remembering that I am
not Van Gogh, that none of my body parts
are extraneous, that if I offer you my breast,
the bone is inseparable. And I wouldn't mind
your teeth on me. If you were so inclined.

Boulder County, September 2013: Upon learning the IUD became dislodged four days after insertion, I thought

a gold microfiber couch may not have been the most practical choice. There's always a mess *somewhere* and a five-year-old everywhere and a leak and a draft and bacon grease and glitter glue and seriously? During my parents' first visit from the swamps of mid-coast Florida *and* the 100-year flood? Because my timing has always been wretched and I never go far enough in malady to merit bed rest and isolation.

Four days prior: *This might get you all the way through to menopause.* Because nothing cheers a woman more than a bridge to shrink the distance between fertility and fallow womb, unless it's a reasonable manifestation of Catholic retribution: of course God will punish me for sexy sex though I supposed his smite would less resemble a small, copper coil dangling from my cervix and appear more like brimstone

                or a flood. Because, really, shouldn't everyone
in Boulder County suffer for my liberated orgasms, not just
my new and somewhat flustered boyfriend weathering nasty
texts about vasectomies and speculums and cramps.
Four days to wait to see if the clinic can fit me
in on Friday, and there's no moral or clever ending. I'm just sad
it won't ever again make sense for me to want a baby.

THE COMPLICATIONS

The question is when will the peaches ripen and where?

We must think about wind storms. How the house
will get cleaned before we go. Who is allowed
to enter. Who is expected to leave.

The patched tire. The neighborhood
watch. Their records and

judgment.

Provisions and resources.
Hydration and storage and sleep.

The child.
The dog.

Which of us must have patience and for what?
Permissible topics of conversation. Public
announcements.

Legalities and ethical implications.
Schedules and biological clocks. Differing
definitions of ripeness. Different

strains.
Temperament.
Expectations.
The optimal route to take.
How high the stakes?

If we get there and the peaches rot?
If we arrive unprepared to manage the pests?

The others who wanted peaches and were turned
away. The question is who will make us suffer?

The question is who will pay for all this
happiness as we make our way?

REVERSIBLE PAPERWORK

I couldn't decide
whether to write about
reversible hats or divorce
paperwork. Seeing how
it is four days before
the new year and
my son's father
is how I now refer
to my husband and
for Christmas I received
a negligee from another
man and seeing how
once when we were dating
my husband changed my
blown out tire and I
latched on to that
kindness and use
its memory to feel
tender at times, like now,
and seeing how any one
of us could die soon
and my son uses his
reversible hat from Peru
as a nest for his stuffed
kitten named Silver,
who is, at this moment,
giving birth to five
babies, and my son
is cooing into that hat
like the Earth's
revolution depends
on it, I sometimes, like
now, wish things could be
undone.

THE REBEL SPEAKS OF HER CREATION

It began in the woods. I entered
the world empty-handed. The new moon
and the old moon fought over
my nocturnal complexion. Things
got ugly. Somewhere a child
was shouting *Mira! La luna,*
la luna! I found her trembling
behind a large boulder. Fruit bats
were caught in her hair. It was me
she was hiding from. No,

                    it began
in a fish market. She entered the world
clutching her sister. The fishmongers
clubbed the sturgeon, squeezed out
the eggs. *What richness* shouted
the brokers. No one noticed
the child lying among the fish
scales, slippery and shimmering.
I held the other already keening
her rage. I cried and cried.
No,

      it began on the rooftop, next
to the dovecote. We entered the world
released. We entered condemned to turn
back. The birds confused us. We gazed
at the sky, stuttering. No,

                    it was a
pigeon coop. No,

            it began in
the barracks. Men wore thick belts
and holsters. Munitions and cartridges.
Triggers and levers, wires and clasps.
We could see no sky from the window.
Aftermath slicked the floor. We waited
for the call of raptors. No one entered

the world. *Not until it is safe,*
my lovelies a soldier whispered
in the dark, one hand fingering
the notches in my skin. No,

                            I can't
remember how it began. Blood
spilled, mapping the dark
like constellations. Again
and again, I sweep flies
from the wound that will not stop
rupturing. The child in my arms.
The flutter of her heart like a bird
escaping. *It began long ago,*
she says. Her fingers skim
puckered scars. *It begins again.*

Notes

Pg 5 – The epigraph is a quote from Getrude Stein's *Tender Buttons*.

Pg 31 – Includes a remix of lyrics from "Let's Get Together" written by Dino Valenti (aka Chet Powers) and recorded by The Kingston Trio (and later, by The Youngbloods).

Pg 49 – *uva*: grape; *cojones*: testicles (slang).

Pg 50 – *la tierra*: land; *vino*: wine.

Pg 51 – *Él fue un mutante*: He was a monster.

Pg 52 – *óvulo*: ovum; *mi hermana*: my sister.

Pg 53 – *tener hambre*: to be hungry; *sangre*: blood.

Pg 54 – *La uva está adentro de la boca de mi hijo*; The grape is inside my son's mouth.

> *La uva es una piedra*: The grape is a stone.

> *la tierra de nuestras ancianas*: our ancestors' land.

Pg 62 – The title and phrase "backwater rising come on" is taken from Alice Notley's *In the Pines*.

Pg 66 – *Mira! La luna, la luna!*; Look! The moon, the moon!

Acknowledgements

I am grateful to the editors of the following magazines and journals in which many of these poems first appeared, sometimes in slightly altered form:

27 rue de fleures, 4th River, Alimentum, American Poetry Review, Anti-, The Awl, The Bakery, Beloit Poetry Journal, Denver Poetry Map, Dusie, Ethel, Everyday Genius, Ilanot Review, Mid-American Review, Mikrokosmos, Misfit Magazine, Nassau Review, NIMROD, Parentheses, Pinyon Poetry Journal, Rattle, Redheaded Stepchild, River City Poetry, Spoon River Poetry Review, Women's Studies Quarterly, Yew

"Lineage" originally appeared as a micro-chapbook (Binge Press). Some poems included in this collection appeared in the chapbook *Slow the Appetite Down* (Spire Press).

Big thanks to Tayve Neese, Sara Lefsyk, and the whole team at Trio House Press for bringing *Waiting for the Wreck to Burn* to life; Sandy Longhorn and Jeff Friedman for seeing something in this book; a multitude of poet-moms and sister-poets who, as a collective force, are *not* to be messed with; Floyd Gabriel, who said Marilyn Sue would have liked the poems; and Henry, for joy, always.

About the Book

Waiting for the Wreck to Burn was designed at Trio House Press through the collaboration of:

Tayve Neese, Lead Editor
Sara Lefsyk, Supporting Editor
Lea C. Deschenes, Interior Design & Cover Design
Jon Bidwell, "Birds and the Blue Sky 02," Cover Photo

The text is set in Adobe Caslon Pro.

The publication of this book is made possible, whole or in part, by the generous support of the following individuals and/or agencies:

Anonymous

About the Press

Trio House Press is a collective press. Individuals within our organization come together and are motivated by the primary shared goal of publishing distinct American voices in poetry. All THP published poets must agree to serve as Collective Members of the Trio House Press for twenty-four months after publication in order to assist with the press and bring more Trio books into print. Award winners and published poets must serve on one of four committees: Production and Design, Distribution and Sales, Educational Development, or Fundraising and Marketing. Our Collective Members reside in cities from New York to San Francisco.

Trio House Press adheres to and supports all ethical standards and guidelines outlined by the CLMP.

Trio House Press, Inc., is dedicated to the promotion of poetry as literary art, which enhances the human experience and its culture. We contribute in an innovative and distinct way to American Poetry by publishing emerging and established poets, providing educational materials, and fostering the artistic process of writing poetry. For further information, or to consider making a donation to Trio House Press, please visit us online at: www.triohousepress.org.

Other Trio House Press Books you might enjoy:

Two Towns Over by Darren C. Demaree
        2017 Trio Award Winner selected by Campbell McGrath

Bird~Brain by Matt Mauch, 2017

Dark Tussock Moth by Mary Cisper
        2016 Trio Award Winner selected by Bhisham Bherwani

Break the Habit by Tara Betts, 2016

Bone Music by Stephen Cramer
        2015 Louise Bogan Award selected by Kimiko Hahn

Rigging a Chevy into a Time Machine and Other Ways
        to Escape a Plague by Carolyn Hembree
        2015 Trio Award Winner selected by Neil Shepard

Magpies in the Valley of Oleanders by Kyle McCord, 2015

Your Immaculate Heart by Annmarie O'Connell, 2015

The Alchemy of My Mortal Form by Sandy Longhorn
        2014 Louise Bogan Winner selected by Carol Frost

What the Night Numbered by Bradford Tice
    2014 Trio Award Winner selected by Peter Campion

Flight of August by Lawrence Eby
    2013 Louise Bogan Winner selected by Joan Houlihan

The Consolations by John W. Evans
    2013 Trio Award Winner selected by Mihaela Moscaliuc

Fellow Odd Fellow by Steven Riel, 2013

Clay by David Groff
    2012 Louise Bogan Winner selected by Michael Waters

Gold Passage by Iris Jamahl Dunkle
    2012 Trio Award Winner selected by Ross Gay

If You're Lucky Is a Theory of Mine by Matt Mauch, 2012